THE

ANNIHILATION OF THE WICKED

SCRIPTURALLY CONSIDERED.

BY REV. W. McDONALD.

The quarrel of the world with Christianity comes to its issue upon the doctrine of future retribution.—ISAAC TAYLOR.

NEW YORK:
NELSON & PHILLIPS.
CINCINNATI: HITCHCOCK & WALDEN.

PREFACE.

"HAS MAN A DUAL NATURE?" During a long and thorough discussion of the foregoing question by, and in the presence of, a large body of Clergymen, the authors of this little volume presented their views upon the subject of the annihilation of the wicked, etc. At the close of the discussion they were unanimously requested, by vote, to publish the same in some convenient form. With such changes as were deemed necessary to adapt them to popular use, they are now offered to the public. The authors do not claim to have furnished an exhaustive treatise on the subject, but a concise statement of the scriptural and philosophical arguments by which this baneful error is overthrown;—a treatise which may be quickly read and easily comprehended by all.

May this little volume lead many, as the discussion did a leading minister of the annihilation faith, to renounce the error and embrace the truth as it is in the word of God.

THE

ANNIHILATION OF THE WICKED.

TO understand the peculiar doctrines of a reformer, we should understand the sentiments of the people among whom he labors.

Jesus came, as he himself declares, (Matt. xv, 13,) to root up every plant which his heavenly Father had not planted. In doing this, he came in direct conflict with the Jews on many questions of faith and practice; exposing their false interpretations of Scripture, and showing that in many things they made void the word of God by their traditions. But upon the question of the existence of *souls* or *spirits*, in distinction from material organization, there appears to be no conflict of sentiment except with the Sadducees, who were the materialists of the time. The Jews, among whom Christ labored, believed in the separate existence of spirits or souls, with endless punishment for the wicked, and happiness of like duration for the righteous. We cannot understand the Old Testament record without admitting that the Hebrews held and taught the doctrine of the immortality of the soul.

1. The fact that a *soul* or *spirit* might exist separate from the body crops out every-where throughout the Old Testament, indicating the belief of the Hebrews.

What other idea could the people receive from Elijah's prayer? "O Lord my God, let this child's soul come into him again; and the Lord heard the voice of Elijah; and the soul of the child came into him again, [or into the midst of him again,] and he revived."

What other meaning could have been inferred from the language of Job? "But his flesh upon him shall have pain, and his soul within him shall mourn."

2. The Jewish belief in *necromancy* is proof of their belief in the separate existence of souls.

They believed that a *necromancer* was one who had power to summon up and consult the dead. The law concerning this practice is in Deut. xviii, 10, 11: "There shall not be found among you any one that maketh his son or his daughter to pass through the fire, or that useth divination, or an observer of times, or an enchanter, or a witch, or a charmer, or a consulter with familiar spirits, or a wizard, or a *necromancer*."

"Necromancers," says Campbell, "are those who consult the dead." Dr. Jahn says: "*Necromancers* pretended that they were able by their incantations to summon back departed spirits from their abodes." Dr. Stackhouse says: "*Necromancy* is the art of raising up the dead in order to pry into future events." Josephus says: "Demons are the spirits of wicked men, who enter into living men and destroy them, unless they are so happy as to meet with speedy relief." It is admitted by our best writers that this was the belief of the Jews.

We have a practical illustration of this belief in the case of Saul, who consulted the witch of Endor. Saul went to this woman with the demand, "Bring me him up whom I shall name unto thee." She did not deny her power to do it, but plead that her life was in danger from Saul's prohibition. On Saul's assuring her that she should not be harmed, she inquired, "Whom shall I bring up unto thee?" He replied, "Bring me up Samuel." Such a request would never have been made had Saul been a materialist. He believed she could call up the spirits of the dead. And in this he but reflected the belief of the Jewish nation.

3. The Jews held the same belief in the time of Christ.

There were at that time three sects among the Jews, namely, the Pharisees, the Sadducees, and the Essenes. The Essenes are not named in the New Testament, for the reason, as it is supposed, that they were an order of the Pharisees, and hence included under that general name.

Of the Pharisees, Josephus says: "They believed that souls have an immortal vigor in them, and that under the earth there will be rewards and punishments according as they have lived virtuously or viciously in this life."—*Ant.*, book xviii, ch. 1, sec. 3. This refers to the intermediate state, or the state of the dead between death and the resurrection.

"They" (the Pharisees) "say that all souls are indestructible," etc. *War*, ii, 14.

Speaking of the Sadducees, Josephus says: "The doctrine of the Sadducees is this: that souls die with the bodies." Again: "They take away the belief in immortality, and the punishments and rewards of hades."

Of the Essenes, Josephus says: "They teach the immortality of souls." "They teach that bodies are corruptible, but that the souls are immortal and continue forever."—*Ant.* xviii, 5; *Wars*, ii, 18, 11. Of the soul, Josephus says: "The soul is ever immortal."

Here is a clear statement of the belief of the Jews in the time of Christ, for the Pharisees embraced the mass of the people. Josephus says, the doctrine of the Sadducees "is received but by few," who, when they became magistrates, "addict themselves to the notions of the Pharisees, because the multitudes would not otherwise hear them."—*Ant.*, xviii, 1, 4.

The testimony of Philo, the Jew, is of value, as indicating the Jewish belief in immortality at that time. Philo was born in Alexandria, Egypt, a few years only before Christ. He says: "Man stands upon the border line of a mortal and immortal nature, participant of each, as was needful, and that he was made at the same time *mortal* and *immortal*—mortal, as to his body; immortal, as to his *mind*." "Death of the man is the separation of the soul from the body; but death of the soul is the *destruction of virtue* and *assumption of vice*."—*Philo Judæus*, i, pp. 32, 65.)

In the New Testament frequent allusions are made to the faith of the Pharisees and Sadducees, with a general disapproval of the doctrines of the latter, and approval of the former.

When Paul stood before the Council at Jerusalem, and perceived that the crowd was composed of Pharisees and Sadducees, he cried out in the Council, "Men and brethren, I am a Pharisee." This announcement produced a dissension between the Pharisees and Sadducees, and divided the multitude. This division was purely doctrinal; "for the Sadducees say that there is no resurrection, neither angels, nor spirits; but the Pharisees confess both." Acts xxii, 8. Paul takes sides here against the Sadducees, who held the doctrine of the non-existence of separate souls. The belief of the Pharisees is made plain also; and they embraced the great mass of the Jewish people. We shall have occasion to refer to this matter again.

Christ's controversy with the Sadducees, mentioned in Matt. xxii, 23; Mark xii, 18; Luke xx, 27, indicates that they were the materialists of his times, answering to the annihilationists of the present day.

The opinions entertained of the Lord Jesus Christ by the Jews, as stated by the disciples, (Matt. xvi, 14,) prove that they believed that the spirits of dead men were still living.

"Whom do men say that I the Son of man

am?" The disciples replied that there was a variety of opinion expressed concerning him. Some said he was John the Baptist; others, that he was Elias; while others claimed that he was Jeremiah; and others still that he was one of the prophets. These men were all dead; and had the Jews believed that dead men ceased to be—had no conscious existence, as materialists believe and teach—they could not have believed that the spirits of these men were present in the person of Jesus Christ. This is a strong argument in favor of the Jewish belief on this question.

If Christ did not believe in the separate, conscious existence of souls after death; if he believed that man ceased to be when he ceased to breathe; that only dust remained—is it not strange, yea, inexplicable, that, living and teaching as he did, among a people the great majority of whom believed in a state of conscious happiness or misery after death, he should not only never oppose such an erroneous theory, but should have employed the same terms which they employed to set forth their obnoxious doctrine; and that, too, without any qualification. Do the advocates of this old Sadducean error keep silent when an opportunity is afforded to defend their peculiar dogma in the presence of those who hold different sentiments?

In speaking of the *state* or *place* of the departed, the Jews called it "a place of darkness." Christ calls it "outer darkness." Matt. xxii, 13. The Jews called it "unquenchable fire." Jesus says, it is "fire that never shall be quenched." Mark ix, 45. The Jews called it "everlasting punishment." Christ says, "These shall go away into everlasting punishment." Matt. xxv, 46. The Jews say, "The just shall obtain an incorruptible and never fading kingdom;" Christ says, "I appoint unto you a kingdom." Luke xxii, 29. The Jews speak of the righteous being "guided with songs, etc., to the right hand, to a place called Abraham's bosom; while the unjust are dragged by force to the left hand, where they are tormented." Christ says, "The beggar died and was carried by the angels into Abraham's bosom." Luke xvi, 22. "And these [the wicked] shall go away into everlasting punishment." The Jews speak of a chaos deep and large, fixed between the good and bad, over which neither the just nor the unjust can pass, if "he were bold enough to attempt it." Christ says, that between the righteous and the wicked there is a "great gulf fixed," etc. Luke xvi, 26.

Now where is the conflict between Christ, the so-called *Annihilationist*, and the great body of the Jewish people who believed in the immortality of the soul, and its separate, conscious existence after death? When he encounters the Sadducees he overturns their doctrine; but the opposite sentiment, held by the Pharisees and Essenes, he approves; and in no instance does he utter one word in condemnation of it.

Admitting that this error, if it be one, is as gigantic and repulsive as its opposers would have us believe—that "it represents our loving God as an implacable tyrant," as one says; that it is "a horrible collection of revolting absurdities;"

that it is "utterly opposed," as says another, "to our natural conceptions of God;" "it staggers the faith of the most devout;" that another calls it "a divine despotism;" another, "the slander of the Almighty;" that it "outrages reason and common sense;" "impeaches God's moral character;" is "the most terrific blasphemy, the most audacious and unmitigated libel ever uttered against a God of love," etc., —admitting, we say, that the doctrine is as horrible as is here described, does it not appear strange that Jesus should have passed it by with so little notice, and especially without disapprobation? that he should have employed terms which must have convinced the Pharisees that he agreed with them, or that he was not opposed to their notions of the soul's immortality, and its existence after death, with eternal rewards and punishments?

Suppose that some advocate of annihilation should enter a city or village where the great mass of the people were believers in what our opponents call "immortal soulism," or the conscious existence of separate souls after death, with unending punishment for the wicked. He is anxious to establish the new faith, and thus correct the errors of the people—errors "utterly opposed to our natural conceptions of God," "the most terrific blasphemy," as well as an "impeachment of God's moral character." The people are assembled, and the preacher of the new faith announces his text—"Matt. xxii, 13: "Bind him hand and foot, and take him away, and cast him into outer darkness; there shall be weeping and gnashing of teeth." In the course of the sermon he repeats, without qualification, such Scriptures as, "Fear not them that kill the body, and after that have no more that they can do. But I will forewarn you whom ye shall fear: Fear him, which, after he hath killed, hath power to cast into hell." Luke xii, 5. "It is better for thee to enter into life halt or maimed, rather than having two hands or two feet to be be cast into everlasting fire," (Matt. xviii, 8,) "where their worm dieth not, and the fire is not quenched." Mark ix, 43, 44.

He speaks of one (the rich man) as actually in hell, tormented in the flames; and another in Abraham's bosom, or paradise, enjoying the good things. He professes to hold conversation with Moses, who had for ages slept in the dust of the earth, etc. Who would conjecture that the preacher was doing more than simply enforcing a doctrine held in common by him and them? Who would imagine that he differed in sentiment from them? Here is Christ preaching to a people who believed in the separate existence of souls—in eternal rewards and punishments—in the conscious state of the dead, and yet, instead of refuting the doctrine and exposing the error of the people, he employs terms which prove in the clearest manner that he does not differ in sentiment from them upon this most important dogma. These considerations lay a foundation for a direct Scriptural argument against the doctrine we here oppose. To this we call the reader's special attention.

With regard to the materialistic doctrine of

the sleep of the dead, and the annihilation of the wicked, there is, as is usual among errorists, a strange want of harmony. On one point, however, they all agree, namely, that *death*, the penalty with which God has threatened sin, *is the absolute extinction of the being of the sinner.* Just when this extinction takes place, whether at death, or at the judgment, or at some subsequent period, they are not agreed.

They all agree in asserting that "*immortality*," by which they mean "eternal life," or simple *being*, is the gift of God by faith in Jesus. By far the greater number of their authorities hold that an extinction of conscious being takes place at death, to be revived at the judgment. A small number only believe that the wicked become extinct at death, and for them remains no resurrection. They hold that man and beast come alike from the "dust;" both have the *same breath*," and both die alike.

They generally believe that the existence of a "soul" or "spirit," as an *entity* separate from the body, is nowhere taught in the Scriptures, and that no conscious soul or spirit survives the death of the body. Upon these points, also, there are differences of opinion among them.

Mr. Zenas Campbell says: "No Scripture or philosophy has ever yet been shown to prove the mind any thing more than an attribute of the living, organized dust; and if so, it must cease with the life of the body."—*Age of Gospel Light*. This being the case, the whole being becomes extinct at death.

Mr. Jacob Blain says: "The Bible plainly tells us that men and beasts are made of the same material—'dust,' and that both have 'the same breath,' and that they both die alike." Again, "The existence of a soul or spirit as an entity within us is only inferred from a few uncertain texts which can be explained another way, while numerous plain texts and the sense of the Bible are against it."—*Death not Life*. Pp. 39, 42.)

Mr. Thomas Reed says: "No conscious spirit

or soul survives the death of man."—*Bible versus Tradition*, p. 121.

Mr. George Storrs is bold, and says: "I regard the phrase 'immaterial' as one which properly belongs to the things which *are not:* a sound without sense or meaning; a mere cloak to hide the nakedness of the theory of an immortal soul in man."—*Six Sermons*, p. 29.

The question at issue being a question of fact, our appeal must be to the word of God. He who made us, and appoints the destiny of all souls, is supposed to be able to impart the most satisfactory information on the subject. And here it is but just to say that our opponents seem to rely less on the word of God than upon other sources of evidence.

Mr. Hudson has produced the most able and elaborate work yet written in defense of this dogma—a volume of 470 pages—and yet only sixty-seven pages of the work are devoted to the Scripture argument, and even these are a medley of Scripture and something else. Subsequently he published a small volume of Scriptural arguments, "to meet," he says, "the convenience of those who rely for their views of future life upon their reading and interpretation of the Scriptures." Then comes a very remarkable confession, with a most humiliating doubt: "We doubt if an exclusively Scriptural argument will prove satisfactory to very many, however clearly it may appear to be made out." —*Christ our Life*, p. 3.

But our appeal is "to the law and to the testimony, for if they speak not according to these, it is because they have no light in them."

Let the reader keep in mind what we have proved, namely, that the Jews, among whom Christ spent his life, believed in the doctrine which our opponents reject, a small sect only dissenting; and with these latter Christ was ever coming in conflict on this peculiar dogma. To have been true to his declared mission (according to our opponents) he should have come in conflict with the great mass of the people. But he not only does not oppose them in this, but employs language well calculated to confirm them in their belief.

I. *The Scriptures make a clear distinction between body and spirit, between the material and immaterial, in man.*

Man, as a physical being, is distinguished from God, as a spirit; from holy angels, and from fallen angels, known as "evil," or "unclean spirits."

God is said to be the "God of the spirits of all flesh." If there be no distinction between "spirit" and "flesh," there can be no sense in such a use of terms.

Job xiv, 22: "But his *flesh* upon him shall have pain, and his *soul* within him shall mourn." Here is the "flesh" without, or "upon him," in "pain," and the "soul within" mourning, and both constituting one man. No language can be more explicit.

Isa. xxxi, 3: "Now the Egyptians are men, and not God; and their horses flesh, and not spirit." If there be any distinction between "men" and "God" in this verse, then there must be a distinction between "flesh" and "spirit."

1 Cor. vi, 20: "Glorify God in your body and in your *spirit*, which are God's." If there be no distinction between "*body*" and "*spirit*," how is this duty to be performed?

2 Cor. iv, 16: "Though our outward man perish, yet the inward man is renewed day by day." The "outward man" can mean only the body; and while that is *perishing* or *decaying*, there is an "inward man" whose vigor is not affected by this *decay* of the body. This "inward man" is the *soul*, which is not dependent upon the body for its vigor.

Jesus appeared to his disciples after his resurrection, (Luke xxiv, 36-40,) and they were "terrified and affrighted, and supposed that they had seen a *spirit*." Seen a spirit! No, never, if they had been *Materialists*. But Jesus disabused their minds: "Behold my hands and my feet, that it is I myself: handle me, and see; for a *spirit* hath not flesh and bones, as ye see me have. And when he had thus spoken, he showed them his hands and his feet."

Mark these facts: 1. That a "*spirit*," which they supposed they had seen, (though *Materialists*, as our opponents claim,) was an entity which had neither "flesh" nor "bones," that is, was not *material*. 2. Christ proves to them that he is not a "*spirit*," by showing them his "hands" and his "feet." Can any thing more clearly prove the distinction between body and spirit?

"Let us cleanse ourselves from all filthiness of the flesh and spirit." 2 Cor. vii, 1.

"Flesh," here, embraces all of man that is *material*, and with Materialists there is nothing else; but with the apostle there *is* something else—a "spirit," or man's immaterial nature.

James ii, 26: "For as the body without the spirit is dead, so faith without works is dead also." The apostle assumes, what was firmly believed at the time, that man is composed of body and spirit. He assumes also that this fact was even better understood than the connection between faith and works. He shows that faith is not saving unless it produces good works, any more than that a body can live without the presence of the spirit. This illustration would have been utterly meaningless had the people believed that body and spirit were included in a single entity.

II. *Any reasoning which would deny to man an immortal or spiritual nature, would deprive God of such a nature, as the same terms are applied to both.*

1. *Let us consider the term soul.* Isa. i, 14. "Your new moons and your appointed feasts my *soul* hateth." This is spoken of God. Deut. vi, 5: "Thou shalt love the Lord thy God, with all thy *soul.*" This is spoken of man. In God the *soul* is the subject of *hatred;* in man it is the subject of *love.* Does "*soul*" mean "spirit" when applied to God, and *body* when applied to man?

"Isa. xlii, 1: "Behold my servant, whom I uphold; mine elect, in whom my *soul* delighteth." This is spoken of God. Isa. lv, 2: "Let your *soul* delight itself in fatness." In these texts the same word is employed to denote the mind of man that is employed to denote the mind of God. Both are represented as the subject of a like passion, which could not be if Materialism be true.

Job xxiii, 13: "What his *soul* desireth, even that he doeth." This is spoken of God. Prov. xxi, 10: "The *soul* of the wicked desireth evil." Here the soul of God and of man are made subjects of a like emotion.

Of God it is said, "Shall not my *soul* be avenged on such a nation as this?" Jer. v, 9. Of man, "Come unto me: hear, and your *soul* shall live." Isa. lv, 3. Now any criticism by which the word *soul* when applied to man is made to mean *life*, *breath*, *wind*, etc., makes with equal force against the spiritual nature of God, and most effectually materializes him. Rev. Dr. Whedon says, "How this denial of the separate existence of pure spirit is saved from materializing God, and so producing either atheism or pantheism, we are not sufficiently read in the system to understand." *Quarterly Review*, January, 1869.

2. *Let us consider the term spirit.* Of God it is said, "The *Spirit* of God moved upon the face of the water." Gen. i, 2. Of man it is said, "The *spirit* of man is the candle of the Lord." Prov. xx, 27.

Of God it is said, "By his *Spirit* he hath garnished the heavens." Job xxvi, 13. Of man it is said, "But there is a *spirit* in man: and the inspiration of the Almighty giveth them understanding." Job xxxii, 8.

Of God it is said, "Whither shall I go from thy *spirit?*" Psa. cxxxix, 17. Of man it is said, "Who knoweth the *spirit* of man that goeth upward?" Eccles. iii, 21.

It is said, "God is a *spirti.*" John iv, 24. Of man it is said, "And the *spirit* shall return unto God who gave it." Eccles. xii, 7.

Stephen prayed, "Lord Jesus, receive my *spirit.*" Of God it is said, "The things of God knoweth no man, but the *Spirit* of God."

No comment is necessary on the foregoing Scriptures, further than to say, that any criticism which will make those Scriptures which apply to man harmonize with the idea that his spirit is an attribute of, or identical with, his material nature, must, to be consistent, involve us in the absurdity of making God material.

There are a class of Scriptures which so connect the spirit of man with the Spirit of God as to prove most conclusively the immateriality of man's nature, or the materiality of the Divine nature.

Rom. viii, 16 : " The Spirit itself beareth witness with our spirit, that we are the children of God." The same word is employed in the original to denote *spirit* in both cases. If by "*our spirit*" is meant our body, or matter, or any material substance, then "*the Spirit*" may mean a material God.

John iv, 24 : " God is a Spirit, and they that worship him must worship him in spirit and in truth." Here the word "*spirit*," being applied to both God and man, proves that both have like qualities of nature. If the text proves that God is *spirit*, and not *matter*, [and if it does not prove this, there is no Scripture which does prove it,] the conclusion must be admitted that man also possesses a nature which is not material.

III. Having proved that man has a soul, or spirit, distinct from matter, we shall proceed to prove that *this soul, or spirit, is not dependent on the body, or matter, for its existence, but may, and does exist separate from it.*

1. Paul believed it possible for the spirit of a man to exist out of the body, or separate from it. 2 Cor. xii, 2–4: "I knew a man in Christ about fourteen years ago, (whether in the body I cannot tell; or whether out of the body I cannot tell; God knoweth:) such a one caught up to the third heaven." On the supposition that Paul was a Materialist; that he believed that the body is the whole of man; that the existence of an entity, as a part of man, capable of existing separate from his body, was an impossibility

—how is his language to be interpreted? Had Paul been a Materialist he must have known whether he was "in the body" or "out of the body." He must have known that to be "out of the body" was an impossibility.

He was "caught up into Paradise, and heard unspeakable words, which it is not lawful for a man to utter." No other interpretation can be given to this than that it teaches the possibility of a spirit not only going "out of the body," but going to the third heaven, even to Paradise; and while there, hearing words not lawful to be repeated here. It proves that Paul believed, if Materialists do not, that he possessed a spirit capable of going out of his body, and existing separate from it.

This has been the ugliest text in the Bible for Materialists to manage; hence their ablest writers generally pass it by in silence. It has never been fairly met; it never can be: for it proves in the most convincing manner the separability of the spirit from the body.

2. 2 Cor. v, 1–8: "For we know that, if our

earthly house of this tabernacle were dissolved, we have a building of God, a house not made with hands, eternal in the heavens. For in this we groan, earnestly desiring to be clothed upon with our house which is from heaven: if so be that being clothed we shall not be found naked. For we that are in this tabernacle do groan, being burdened: not for that we would be unclothed, but clothed upon, that mortality might be swallowed up of life. . . . Therefore we are always confident, knowing that, whilst we are at home in the body, we are absent from the Lord. . . . We are confident, I say, and willing rather to be absent from the body, and to be present with the Lord." On the supposition that *spirit* and *body* are one, what does Paul mean by "at home in the body," and "absent from the body?" What is meant by putting off "this tabernacle," and being "clothed with our house which is from heaven?" To be with Christ is to be "absent from the body." But to be "absent from the body" is an impossibility, according to Materialism; hence, nothing is gained by laying off "this tabernacle." In fact there is no such thing as laying off "this tabernacle;" for the "*I*" or "*We*" who does it is simply the "tabernacle" laid off, according to Materialists. It is the house or tabernacle taking itself down.

3. Phil. i, 21–24: "For to me to live is Christ, and to die is gain. But if I live in the flesh, this is the fruit of my labor: yet what I shall choose I wot not. For I am in a strait betwixt two, having a desire to depart, and to be with Christ; which is far better. Nevertheless to abide in the flesh is more needful for you." Who that has not a favorite creed to support would ever conclude that this declaration could fall from the lips of a Materialist? How death, or non-being, could be gain to a man who was treasuring up, by his "light afflictions," a "far more exceeding and eternal weight of glory," we are unable to determine. Where is the earnest Christian who would not prefer labor for Christ to sleep, or non-being? He is not worthy of the Christian name who prefers the sluggard's sleep

to earnest labor. Abiding "in the flesh" means living in the body. "To depart" means simply going out of the body; and going out, or away from the body, is to "be with Christ." Had Paul been a Materialist, or an Annihilationist, he must have known that to "abide in the flesh" for the salvation of sinners and the good of the Church would not have delayed the period of his being with Christ one hour; for, according to the doctrine of our opponents, he is not with Christ even to this present time. He could have continued his labors until he was as old as Methuselah, and then be with Christ just as soon as though he had died that day. How could he have desired to depart and be with Christ, unless being with Christ was to be the result of that departure? Yet, if the doctrine we oppose be true, that result was not hastened one moment by his departure. This text has accordingly annoyed our opponents. They confess that "a fair construction of this text" would be that Paul "expected to be with Christ immediately on his departure." But they think that there are Scriptures against it; hence the "fair construction" of the text must not be accepted.

IV. Paul avows his belief *not only in the resurrection of the dead, both of the just and unjust, but in the existence of "angels and spirits."*

1. Acts xxiii, 6: "But when Paul perceived that the one part were Sadducees, and the other Pharisees, he cried out in the council, Men and brethren, I am a Pharisee, the son of a Pharisee."

This profession of Paul produced a dissension between the Sadducees and the Pharisees. The cause of this dissension is said to be this: "For the Sadducees say that there is no resurrection, neither angel nor spirit: but the Pharisees confess both." On this announcement, the Scribes, who were of the Pharisees, arose and took Paul's part, saying, "We find no evil in this man." They declare what seems to be a clear confirmation of their belief in angels and spirits. "But if a spirit or an angel hath spoken to him, let us not fight against God."

What is meant here by "angels" and "spirits" is not difficult to understand. Mr. Barnes has the following comment on the passage: "*Neither angel*—That there are no angels. They deny the existence of good and bad angels. *Nor spirit*—Or *soul*. They held that there was nothing but matter. They were Materialists, and supposed that all the operations which we ascribe to mind could be traced to some modification of matter."

As we have before shown, the controversy between the Pharisees and the Sadducees embraced two points—the "resurrection of the dead," and the existence of "angels and spirits." Paul here publicly professes to be of those who held the anti-materialistic view of souls and spirits; turning a cold shoulder to those who advocated a doctrine, to the spread of which he had devoted his life, provided he were a Materialist. There is no way to interpret the apostle's averments in this case with a shade of consistency, without admitting that he held the doctrine of the separate existence of *spirits* or *souls*.

V. Christ's controversy with the Sadducees (Luke xx, 37) is a defense of the same doctrine. "Now that the dead are raised, even Moses showed at the bush, when he calleth the Lord the God of Abraham, and the God of Isaac, and the God of Jacob. For he is not a God of the dead, but of the living: for all live unto him." Matt. xxii, 31, 32. When God made this announcement at Horeb with regard to Abraham, Isaac, and Jacob, the last named had been dead about 200 years; and yet God declares that he *is* their God. Christ adds: "He is not a God of the dead, but of the living." Then, to make the doctrine of universal application, he is careful to add, "All live unto him;" as much as to say, Not only are "Abraham, Isaac, and Jacob" living, but the statement is true of "*all* men." Logically, the argument would stand thus: He is not the God of the dead, but of the living. He is the God of Abraham, of Isaac, and of Jacob; therefore Abraham, Isaac, and Jacob must be living. Let it be remembered that the Sadducees believed that the whole man became extinct at death; that neither soul nor body would ever be reproduced. With them the immortality of the soul, or spirit, and the resurrection of the dead, stood or fell together.

To prove that the soul existed after death was to silence their objections to the resurrection of the body. It was necessary, therefore, in a discussion with the Sadducees, to prove the separate existence of spirits, in order to prove the resurrection of the dead. As there could be no resurrection unless the soul maintained a conscious existence after death, and as the Sadducees denied such conscious existence, it was necessary for Christ to prove it, in order to lay a proper foundation for a belief in the resurrection of the dead.

The fact that Christ, all through his ministry, sided with the Pharisees against the Sadducees, who were the Materialists of his times, is an argument against Materialism not easily answered.

VI. Christ's language to the dying thief, (Luke xxiii, 43,) "To-day shalt thou be with me in Paradise," *is one of the strongest proofs of the conscious existence of soul after the death of the body.*

We will not detain the reader with any criticisms on "Paradise," or on the attempts of Materialists to change the sense of this text, by changing the pointing. It is only necessary to say that this last method is arrant nonsense. As to the location of "Paradise," we need only say that it must be in or near the "third heaven," where people do not sleep, as Paul heard *words* there "not lawful to be uttered."

But how, it may be asked, could the thief be in Paradise that day with Christ when three days later he declares, "I am not yet ascended?"

This question may be satisfactorily answered.

1. As a *Divine being*, Christ was in Paradise that day. He says, "the Son of man is in heaven." John iii, 13.

2. As a *disembodied spirit* he might have been in Paradise that day. For, before his body was placed in Joseph's tomb, he had said,

"Father, into thy hands I commit my spirit; and having said this, he gave up the ghost."

3. But as a *risen* Saviour he had not ascended. His ascension did not take place until many days after the crucifixion. So as a Divine being, and as a disembodied spirit, Christ could have been with the thief that day in Paradise, and yet, as a risen, glorified Saviour, not have ascended until some forty days later. This interpretation makes the Scripture both plain and simple.

VII. Take the case of the appearance of Moses on the Mount of Transfiguration.

Moses died in the land of Moab, and was buried in a valley over against Bethpeor, etc., (Deut. xxxiv, 5, 6;) and yet, nearly fifteen hundred years after he had become *extinct*—had ceased to be, soul and body, according to Materialists, he appears on Mount Tabor with him who had gone to heaven in a chariot of fire.

There is not the slightest evidence that Moses was raised from the dead for this special purpose. Materialists say, that if Moses did really appear—of which they have serious doubts—he was raised from non-being for that special purpose, and after he had performed his mission was sent back again to non-existence, to be known and to know no more until the general resurrection. If this be so, Moses must have possessed a spirit of submission beyond most men, or he would have plead earnestly to have been spared another two or three thousand years' slumber. Then, how this idea of Moses's resurrection is to be harmonized with the fact that Christ is the "first-fruits" of the resurrection, Materialists have not been kind enough to inform us. Here is the spirit of one whose body had slumbered in a grave, in the land of Moab, for fifteen hundred years, standing on Mount Tabor, seen of the favored three, and conversing with Jesus concerning his *passion;* proving beyond all cavil that the soul lives after the body is dead.

VIII. We urge the following additional arguments against the doctrine of Annihilation.

1. It makes no distinction between the state of a sinner before and after the resurrection, raising him from a state of non-existence to consign him to the same state again.

A large majority of those who believe in the final annihilation of the wicked, believe also in a resurrection, "both of the just and of the unjust." But why raise the wicked from a state of *unconscious*, if not *absolute, non-being*, to consign them to the same state again? Many Annihilationists, not being able to see the reason for this, reject, consistently, we think, the doctrine of the resurrection of the wicked altogether.

2. The doctrine makes no distinction in regard to the *degrees* of punishment—a doctrine clearly set forth in the word of God.

Rev. George Storrs says, (*Herald of Life*,) "As to degrees of punishment in a future state we challenge the evidence in the word of God of any such thing. It is purely a human speculation."

We will let the word of God speak for itself. Christ says of the "Scribes and Pharisees, hypocrites," "Ye shall receive the greater damnation." Matt. xxiii, 14. Does not this teach that there are *degrees* of "damnation" for the wicked? If there are no *degrees* of damnation it would be impossible for it to be "*greater*" in one case than in another.

Luke xii, 47, 48: "And that servant, which knew his lord's will, and prepared not himself, neither did according to his will, shall be beaten with many stripes. But he that knew not, and did commit things worthy of stripes, shall be beaten with few stripes. For unto whomsoever much is given, of him shall be much required; and to whom men have committed much, of him they will ask the more." Do not the "many" and the "few stripes" clearly prove that there are degrees of punishment?

When the Scriptures speak of receiving according to the "deeds done in the body," and "according to their works"—when they represent that it will be "more tolerable in the day of judgment" for one class of sinners than for another—he must be blinded by his *dogma-*

God, who is not able to see degrees of punishment for the unsaved.

There are no degrees in annihilation; consequently, if that be the penalty for sin it will fall on all alike; but as punishment will not fall on all alike, annihilation cannot be the penalty for sin.

3. This doctrine makes death the extreme penalty of the law, in opposition to the Scriptures, which speak of a "much sorer punishment" than death for those who do "despite unto the Spirit of grace."

Heb. x, 28, 29: "He that despised Moses's law died without mercy under two or three witnesses: of how much sorer punishment, suppose ye, shall he be thought worthy, who hath trodden under foot the Son of God, and hath counted the blood of the covenant, wherewith he was sanctified, an unholy thing, and hath done despite unto the Spirit of grace?"

Death, which, our opponents say, is capital punishment—and hence the extreme penalty of the law—was inflicted "without mercy" on those "who despised Moses's law." They received, say Annihilationists, by being blotted out of being, all the punishment it was possible for them to receive. But we are informed by Paul that there is a *sorer* or *worse* punishment than even death for those who reject Christ, and trample under foot the Son of God, and count his blood an unholy thing.

Mr. Storrs attempts to dispose of this argument in the following manner. He says, "This objection is founded on one solitary text, and that misconstrued. The Syriac version, translated by Prof. Murdock, formerly of the Andover Theological Institute, reads, 'How much more, think ye, will he receive capital punishment,' etc., instead of *sorer;* making the greater *certainty* of the death punishment."—*Herald of Life*, March 10, 1869.

This is a very remarkable authority. Instead of consulting the original, or some authorized translation, Mr. Storrs resorts to a translation of a translation—Prof. Murdock's translation of the Syriac translation—and by this attempts to disprove the doctrine of the Authorized Version. But Mr. Storrs must know that the word rendered "*sorer*," has no such meaning as "*much more*," or "*more certain*." Χειρον, (*cheiron*,) according to Robinson, means *worse*, spoken of a *state* or *condition:* of *punishment*, as *worse*, *more severe*. It is from κακος—*bad*, *ill*, *evil*—and never has the sense of *more certain*, or *much more*.

If we consult the New Testament use of the word we shall find that no such meaning is given to it as Mr. Storrs forces out of his second-hand translation. With the exception of Heb. x, 29, the word is invariably rendered *worse*.

Matt. ix, 16: "No man putteth a piece of new cloth unto an old garment; for that which is put in to fill it up taketh from the garment, and the rent is made (*cheiron*) *worse*;" that is, according to Mr. Storrs, *much more certain* than before mended.

Matt. xii, 45: "The last state of that man is (*cheirona*) *worse* than the first;" that is, *much more certain*. He is more certain to have an end than a beginning. But how the taking of seven other spirits more wicked than himself could make such a result more certain we are not informed.

Matt. xxvii, 64: "So the last error shall be (*cheiron*) *worse* than the first;" that is, *much more certain.*

Mark v, 26: "And had suffered many things of many physicians, and had spent all that she had, and was nothing bettered, but rather grew (*cheiron*) *worse*," that is, *much more certain.* Much more certain than what?

John v, 14: "Behold, thou art made whole: sin no more, lest a (*cheiron*) *worse* thing come unto thee;" that is, a *much more certain* thing. How a much more certain thing could come upon him than the "thirty and eight years'" infirmity, we are not told. But how a *worse thing* could come upon him we can easily understand.

2 Pet. ii, 20: "For if after they have escaped the pollutions of the world through the knowledge of the Lord and Saviour Jesus

Christ, they are again entangled therein, and overcome, the latter end is (*cheirona*) *worse* than the beginning," that is, *much more certain*. How the last or latter end of a man can be *worse* than the beginning is not difficult to understand; but how it can be *more certain* will require the logic of Mr. Storrs, or some other Annihilationist, to make plain.

1 Tim. v, 8: "But if any provide not for his own, and especially for those of his own house, he hath denied the faith, and is (*cheiron*) *worse* than an infidel," that is, *much more certain* than an infidel.

2 Tim. iii, 13: "But evil men and seducers shall wax worse and worse, deceiving, and being deceived;" that is, *doubly certain*, amounting to a terrible certainty.

Ordinary discernment, coupled with common honesty, will discover the utter fallacy, not to say unpardonable wickedness, of all such attempts to wrest the Scriptures for the purpose of sustaining a favorite dogma.

4. The doctrine of annihilation makes the

punishment of the wicked to consist in simple *non-existence*, in direct opposition to those Scriptures which represent it as *conscious suffering*.

Mr. Storrs says, "The Bible affirms the wages of sin is *death*, and nowhere represents the punishment of the wicked in the future life to be conscious suffering."—*Herald of Life*, May 10, 1869. Let us inquire what the Scriptures do teach on this important subject.

Matt. xxv, 30: "Cast ye the unprofitable servant into outer darkness: there shall be weeping and gnashing of teeth."

Luke xiii, 28: "There shall be weeping and gnashing of teeth, when ye shall see Abraham, and Isaac, and Jacob, and all the prophets, in the kingdom of God, and you yourselves thrust out."

Luke xvi, 23: "And in hell he lifted up his eyes, being in torments."

Rom. ii, 8, 9: "Indignation and wrath, tribulation and anguish, upon every soul of man that doeth evil; of the Jew first, and also of the Gentile."

Luke xii, 47: "And that servant which knew his lord's will, and prepared not himself, neither did according to his will, shall be beaten with many stripes."

Luke xvi, 24: "Send Lazarus, that he may dip the tip of his finger in water, and cool my tongue; for I am tormented in this flame."

Mark ix, 44: "Where their worm dieth not, and the fire is not quenched."

These Scriptures relate to the punishment of the wicked. If "weeping and gnashing of teeth;" if "being in torments;" if "tribulation and anguish;" if being "beaten with many stripes;" if being "tormented in this flame;" if "their worm dieth not"—if all these do not teach conscious suffering, they do not teach any thing relating to suffering. If the penalty of the law be annihilation, conscious suffering is excluded. But conscious suffering is not excluded; therefore, annihilation is not the penalty of the law.

5. The doctrine of annihilation makes the sufferings of the wicked terminate at death, or,

at most, at the judgment, in opposition to the Scriptures, which represent them as eternal. Mr. Storrs says, "Nowhere is there an assertion in the Bible that represents the conscious suffering of the wicked to be eternal."

Let it be remembered that Annihilationists hold that the punishment of the wicked, whatever it may be, is eternal. "Death holds them," says Mr. Storrs, "in its eternal dominion; they shall never live again." He says again: "It is an unbroken death state that is the punishment." The only question to be settled is, Is that state one of mere non-existence, or is it a conscious state?

All punishment must consist either in *pain*, or *loss*, or *both*. As Annihilationists exclude the idea of *pain*, the penalty of the law, in their view, must consist simply and solely in *loss*. But what is it the loss of? not of pleasure, for of that the sinner has none while out of Christ. It must be the loss of simple existence. But the loss of simple existence, under the circumstances, cannot be an evil to a sinner—a punishment—

but a great blessing. Punishment must be the loss of what, to a sinner, is valuable, or it is no punishment. But existence to a sinner, instead of being valuable, is a positive evil, and, consequently, to be deprived of it is no punishment. "To cease to exist cannot be punishment of loss, only so far as the existence taken away involves happiness; but the existence of sinners, who shall be such after the resurrection, will not involve happiness, but misery; and therefore to cease to exist will not involve a loss of happiness, but an exemption from suffering, and cannot be a penalty or punishment."—*Lee's Theology*, p. 326.

The term "punishment," according to the best English authority, means "pain or suffering inflicted on a person for a crime or offense." "To afflict with pain, loss, or calamity, for a crime or fault." "To chastise." "To reward with pain or suffering," etc.—*Webster*.

The Greek word *κολασιν*, *kolasin*, from *kolazo*, signifies "*chastisement*, *punishment*, *torment*, *torture*," etc. The English and the Greek terms, in their significations, are as far removed from the idea of annihilation as light is from darkness. To *chastise*, *torment*, *afflict with loss*, cannot be affirmed of those who have ceased to be, but of those who possess conscious existence.

As, then, the punishment of the wicked, whatever it may be, is confessed by Annihilationists to be eternal, the conclusion is irresistible, that it must be endless conscious suffering.

6. The doctrine of annihilation stamps as a deception all the horrors of the wicked, as well as the blissful hopes of the righteous at death.

Hear the dying Altamont: "This body is all weakness and pain; but my soul, as if strung up by torment to greater strength and spirit, is full powerful to reason; full mighty to suffer. And that which triumphs in the jaws of mortality is doubtless immortal." "Didst thou feel half the mountain that is on me, thou wouldst struggle with the martyr for his stake, and bless heaven for the flames: that is not an everlasting flame; that is not an unquenchable fire."

Said an English nobleman on his death-bed, "It is not giving up my breath, it is not being for ever insensible, at which I shrink; it is the *terrible hereafter*—the *something beyond* the *grave*—at which I recoil." The last hours of Paine, Voltaire, Chesterfield, and others, prove that before apostates and enemies of Christ close their probation, God permits them to see the coming torments which await them in the world of woe.

Stephen, when dying, instead of looking into the grave, where, according to Annihilationists, he must remain unconscious for ages, looks up steadfastly into heaven, and sees Jesus at the right hand of God; and, while gazing upon His ineffable glory, his face became shining like that of an angel, and he cried, "Lord Jesus, receive my spirit!" Where? Not where Jesus was not, but where he was, namely, "in heaven, at the right hand of God." As died Stephen, so die good men.

When Dr. Fisk was dying, as he was being moved from his chair he exclaimed, "From the chair to the throne!" Instead of the throne, was it to be the sleep of ages in the grave?

Rev. William Grimshaw, a few moments before his death, being asked by a friend how he was, said: "I am as happy as I can be on earth, and as sure of glory as if I was in it. I have nothing to do but to step out of this bed into heaven. I have my feet on the threshold already." Were these heaven-inspired hopes to be rewarded with unconscious existence in the grave for a period to mortals unknown?

Dr. Payson said, when about to die, "It seems as if my soul had found a pair of new wings, and was so eager to try them that, in her fluttering, she would rend the fine net-works of the body to pieces." Were these holy men deceived? Did God open heaven to their vision only to close it and send them to the sleep of ages? Instead of their feet resting on the threshold of the city of God, ready to enter, were they only standing at the grave's mouth, which was to be the home of their spirits for ages? Were their immortal songs, sung so sweetly at the door of the eternal mansion, to be hushed in the sleep of ages? God never deceives his children thus.

7. The doctrine we oppose is a prime doctrine of infidelity, and should be rejected by every Christian.

We can but regret that men who claim to love God and believe in Jesus should be aiding, as we believe they are, the Prince of darkness in forwarding his designs to ruin men, by lessening the force of the Divine threatenings against sin. Isaac Taylor has very justly said: "The quarrel of the world with Christianity comes to its issue upon this doctrine of future retribution."—*Sat. Night*, p. 219. Speaking of Democritus and Epicurus, Plutarch says, "They taught that the soul is corruptible, and perishes with the body." It is known that Epicurus taught that the soul comes from a material source, exists in a material system, is nourished by material food, grows and is matured with the material body, and declines with its decline, and hence must die when it dies.—*Landes.* He was a most determined foe of the doctrine of immortality. Bayle speaks of their theory thus: "Death disunites the parts of these bodies, but destroys nothing of their substance. Those that the earth supplies are restored to the earth, and those which descend from the regions of ether, ascend thither again." In a work by Ellis and Reed, ("*Bible versus Tradition*,") they say on Eccles. xii, 7: "The *ruah* [spirit] goes to God who gave it. Now if God intends to restore this *ruah* to the man so that he may *live again*, where does God bring this *ruah* from? We shall see that it is not the *same ruah*, but *ruah* of the *same kind*, though perhaps less diluted with *atmospheric air*." 'Thus we see that it is God's *ruah*—one universal principle pervading the *atmosphere*." "It is a living thing, though the cause of life, but which our honest translators have translated wind."

Zenas Campbell says, "No Scripture or philosophy has ever yet been shown to prove the mind any thing more than an attribute of the living organized dust; and if so, it must cease with the life of the body."—*Age of Gospel Light.* How do these views differ from those of Epicurus?

Eusebius, who lived in the third century, and wrote the first "History of the Primitive Church," after the Acts of the Apostles, in speaking of the heretics of his times says, "But about this time, also, other men sprang up in Arabia, as the propagators of false opinions. These asserted that the human soul, as long as the present state of the world existed, perished at death, and died with the body, but that it would be raised again with the body at the time of the resurrection. And as a considerable council was held on account of this, Origen being again requested, likewise here discussed the point in question with so much force, that those who had before been led astray, completely changed their opinion."—P. 253.

Voltaire says, (*Phil. Dic.*, vol. i, pp. 42–48,) "My being rewarded or punished after death requires that something which feels and thinks in me must continue to subsist after me. Now as no part in me has any thought or sense before my birth, why should it after my death? What can this incomprehensible part of myself be? Will the humming of the bee continue after the end of its existence? Thus the soul itself, which signifies our *memory*, *our reason*, our *passions*, is only a bare word.

"How can I be rewarded or punished when I shall cease to be myself, when nothing which constituted my person will be remaining?"

Volney, in his "*Ruins*," says, "The soul is but the vital principle which results from the *properties of matter*, and from the action of the elements in these bodies, where they create a spontaneous movement. To suppose that this product of the play of the organs, born with them, matured with them, and which sleep with them, can subsist when they cease, is the romance of a wandering imagination."

When Abner Kneeland, in 1824, was half way between Universalism and Infidelity, he published a volume of lectures, in which he says, "Although the consequence of death would have been eternal had it not been for eternal life, yet the consequence would not have been eternal misery, but an eternal extinction of being: for death is an extinction of life."

"It will be perceived that the author does not believe in an intermediate state of conscious existence between death and the resurrection, and of course death to him is an extinction of being, and all his ideas of a future state of existence are predicated on the glorious doctrine of the resurrection."—P. 48.

Mr. Balfour says, "No sacred writer mentions an immortal soul." "There is no *immaterial*, *immortal* soul which lives in a conscious state of happiness or misery in a disembodied condition."

We see by these references that Annihilationists have taken up the dogma regarded as fundamental by these old enemies of Christianity, and have adopted it as a primal doctrine of their creed, and exhibit a zeal in its propagation far exceeding that of its hoary-headed and corrupt authors. We regret that our opponents are found in such company, for we believe them, in this particular, to be far better than their creed would indicate.

We notice, in closing our brief examination of this strange dogma, two objections urged by its advocates. The first we denominate

Conditional Immortality.

This may be regarded as the nucleus of the theory. The term "*immortality*," it is claimed, has the sense of simple *existence*, and not a *state* or *condition* of existence.

The argument is stated as follows:

1. God alone possesses immortality, (1 Tim. vi, 16,) meaning eternal existence.

2. Man is required to seek immortality, (Rom. ii, 7,) meaning simple existence.

3. It is claimed that immortality is the gift of Christ as Redeemer, and dependent on the resurrection.

Let us examine these statements. The first fact stated is, that God only, or alone, hath immortality; and, if possessed by man, it must be conferred by the grace of Christ. The immortality possessed by God only, at the time the apostle made this announcement, will, it seems, ultimately be possessed by all the saints, and then it will no longer be said, "God only hath immortality." But is it true, according to the views of Annihilationists that God *was* the only being in the universe at that time who possessed immortality? If we are not mistaken, at the time Paul made this announcement, some, in their sense, were already possessed of immortality. Enoch and Elijah, at least, were immortal in their sense; so that God at that time was not the only being in the universe who possessed immortality.

The apostle's statement, "God only hath immortality," will remain true to all eternity. It is generally admitted that the term, as here employed, means an *underived existence*, in such a sense as no mere creature can or will ever possess it, however earnestly he seeks it. But when applied to man, it signifies that he is not liable to corruption or decay. With God it is *underived;* with man it is *derived.* The two immortalities differ widely.

The term is employed also to describe the believer's crown—"*incorruptible.*" It is applied to the resurrection body—"*raised in incorruption.*" It is employed also to describe the believer's inheritance—"*incorruptible.*" And yet, "God only hath immortality."

The second fact stated is, that man is required to seek immortality, which would not be if all men possessed it.

In the sense of "immortal inheritance" and "crown of life," immortality is conditional. But this is not simple existence, as Annihilationists claim, but ineffable happiness, which all men may accept or refuse. It is not immortality abstractly, but a *blessed* immortality. To illustrate: there is a sense in which we are required to seek the resurrection of the dead, (Phil. iii, 7–11,) and yet we are assured that all men—"the just and the unjust"—shall be raised. No one will claim that the resurrection, in the abstract, is to be sought, but simply a *blessed* resurrection, or "a better resurrection," as the Scriptures describe it. In like manner there is a sense in which immortality is to be sought; and yet there is a sense in which all men will possess it. As mere existence, without reference to the character of that existence, immortality is possessed by all; but as a *blessed* existence it is possessed only by those who seek it by faith in Christ.

The third fact stated is, that immortality is the gift of Christ as Redeemer.

That we owe our entire existence to Christ as *Creator*, will not be denied; but that we owe our existence to him as *Redeemer*, is a pure assumption. It would be just as proper to say that our material bodies came by Christ as Redeemer, as to say that our immortal spirits came by him. Christ, as Redeemer, has but one work, that of saving sinners from their sins, and preparing them for a blissful immortality.

The second objection we denominate

THE DEATH AND DESTRUCTION ARGUMENT.

That God has the power to blot from being all things and beings created by him, there can be no doubt; but that he will do it, there is no evidence in the word of inspiration.

1. The terms "*life*" and "*death*" are frequently employed by Annihilationists. "Life," with them, signifies *simple existence*, and "*death*," *cessation* or *extinction* of *existence*, or *being*. "Death," being the penalty of the law, its infliction upon sinners is the blotting of them out of being. "Life," being the gift of God to believers in Christ, its bestowment is simply the gift of *being*.

Now we deny that such is the exclusive meaning of these terms. Take the term "*death*." In some instances you cannot force extinction, or even suspension of vitality or existence, out of it. Jesus says: "Except a corn of wheat fall into the ground and *die*, it abideth alone; but if it *die*, it bringeth forth much fruit." Paul says:

"That which thou sowest is not quickened except it *die.*" Here the term death has its ordinary signification. But instead of the annihilation of being, its vitality is not even suspended; for through the whole process of *death* the living germ retains its vital power unharmed. The outer coat molders away, but the principle of life is still vital and active. If the corn can stand the infliction of this death penalty without a suspension of its vitality, may not the spiritual nature of man endure it without annihilation?

Lazarus *died*, and, instead of ceasing to be, he was carried into Abraham's bosom. The rich man *died*, and, instead of being annihilated, he is lifting up his eyes "in hell, being in torment." To say that "the wages of sin is death," is not saying that the wages of sin is annihilation. Death is used to express separation from holiness. "And you hath he quickened, who were dead in trespasses and sins." "Thou hast a name that thou livest and art dead." "For this my son was dead, and is alive again." Death cannot, in these instances, mean extinction of conscious being, or annihilation.

The use of the term "life" by Annihilationists is equally unscriptural. They never make any more out of it than *simple being*, while the Scriptures represent it as *well being*, or blessedness. When Joseph says, "God did send me before you to preserve life," nothing more is meant than simple being. But when Christ says, "If thou wilt enter into life, keep the commandments," he means, not simple being, but the blessedness of salvation.

When Jesus commands, "Take no thought for your life," he is not to be understood as exhorting them to take no thought for salvation. But when he says, "Ye will not come unto me that ye might have life," he does mean the blessedness of salvation.

These Scriptures indicate the use of the term "*life*." And yet Annihilationists constantly employ this term to signify exclusively simple existence.

2. Take the terms "*destroy*" and "*perish*."

Annihilationists claim that these terms, applied to human beings, mean extinction of being, or annihilation. But if this be the meaning of these terms, then the Scriptures teach not only the extinction of the wicked, but of all men, good and bad.

Job says, (xxxiv, 15,) "All flesh shall *perish* together." As the "*flesh*," or body, is all there is of man, if materialism be true, and as "*all flesh*" must mean all human beings, this text of necessity proves the utter extinction or annihilation of the whole race. And Job is careful to include the good in the list. He says, (ix, 22,) "He destroyeth the *perfect* and the *wicked*." This puts an end to the whole race. Materialists are not relieved by the resurrection of the just, for there can be no resurrection. God says of the Babylonians, (Jer. li, 39,) they shall "sleep a perpetual sleep, and not wake." David is bold, and says, (Psa. lxxxviii, 5,) "Free among the dead, like the slain that lie in the grave, whom thou rememberest no more." If this sleep is to be perpetual, if the sleepers are never "to wake," and are no more to be remembered, even by the Almighty, then there is no resurrection, at least for sinners. But as no distinction is made between saint and sinner, the saint will never awake; for "he," be he good or bad, "that goeth down to the grave shall come up no more." Job vii, 9. "I go whence I shall not return, even to the land of darkness and the shadow of death." Job x, 21. "Mine eye shall no more see good." Job vii, 7.

We repeat, if the Babylonians were to sleep a perpetual sleep, and not wake; if God was to remember the wicked no more; if the dead were never to arise and praise God; if those who went down to the grave were to come up no more; if a very good man was never to return from the land of darkness, and no more to see good; if the perfect and the wicked were to be alike destroyed, and all flesh were to perish together—that is, according to Materialists, to be annihilated—what is the hope for the race? Who is to be saved?

When Annihilationists ring their changes on

"The dead know not any thing," and regard that as the end of all controversy with regard to the conscious state of the dead, they should not stop there, but repeat the rest of the verse, "neither have they any more a reward." That would put an end to the whole matter, which would be perfectly satisfactory to every Deist and Atheist in the land; for if by, "The dead know not any thing," is meant the unconscious state of the dead, then "neither have they any more a reward" must mean that they are never to be raised to life eternal. If there be any doubt as to the meaning of the text named, the following must settle it forever—"He that goeth down to the grave shall come up no more."

It is very evident, from what has been said, that "destruction" and "perish" do not mean annihilation. *Destroy* is often used to signify simply physical death: "But the chief priests and elders persuaded the multitude that they should ask Barabbas, and *destroy* Jesus." Did they contemplate the annihilation of Jesus? The Jews did not believe in annihilation. The word *destroy* is frequently used to signify the ruin of a thing or person, and not their annihilation. "My people are destroyed for lack of knowledge." "He hath destroyed me on every side." "O Israel, thou hast destroyed thyself; but in me is thine help."

There is no Scripture proof that the word "perish" ever signifies annihilation. It is sometimes used to express a violent death. "From the blood of Abel unto the blood of Zacharias, which *perished* between the altar and the temple." But its most common meaning is, the ruin of a thing or person: "And the bottles *perish*," (Matt. ix, 17,) are ruined, but not annihilated.

When Jeremiah predicted that the land of Judea should *perish*, and be burned up, (Jer. ix, 12,) he did not look to see it annihilated, but simply ruined. In this last sense the word is employed when used to express the penalty of sin; it simply means that the sinner is ruined.

Finally, the Scriptures are clear on the subject of the sinner's future state as being one of banishment from the presence of God, united with conscious suffering, and both to continue forever. "O that men were wise," that they would consider this, and seek an immortality of glory, and escape indignation and wrath—not annihilation—which cometh "upon every soul of man that doeth evil!"

THE TWOFOLD NATURE OF MAN PSYCHOLOGICALLY CONSIDERED.

BY REV. W. R. CLARK, D.D.

A CLASS of Biblicists deny the immateriality of the human soul. The facts of psychology, it is alleged, require a modification of the commonly received interpretation of the Bible upon this subject, as the facts of astronomy and geology have compelled other modifications of Scripture exegesis. A sensitive nerve is this, and touched by those who are even warmly attached to the Bible as their infallible guide. Their error may be detected by a little careful attention to the following points:

1. *Man's personal identity.* This is one of his indestructible ideas, like those of personal existence, space, or duration. He can no more believe that he is not the same person to-day

that he was yesterday or last year, than that he does not exist in space.

Further, he is shut up to this conviction by the *reductio ad absurdum.* It is an established fact that the body is constantly changing by waste and supply, so that within a few months, or years at farthest, every particle of the former body passes away. If man is composed of nothing but a material body, then the totality of his former self passes away with this change; he is a new creature in such a sense that his present self can no more be responsible for the acts of his former self than for the acts of any other being.

Suppose him arraigned at court for a crime committed seven years ago; he has only to adduce the change of identity effected by the entire displacement of the particles composing the body which committed the crime to establish an *alibi.* The jury must then either acquit him, or deny the physiological facts adduced, or assume his duality.

Again, this hypothetical change of identity

requires that marriage be resolemnized as often as the particles of the bodies which covenanted in the former ceremony are entirely displaced. And no parents can have lineal descendants over seven years of age; beyond that period the children bearing their names are theirs only by adoption, as might be any other "little wanderers."

But a graver difficulty is that which involves the Divine administration in injustice in bringing man to an account for *all* the deeds done in the body, when the person so called to his account can only be the author of the deeds done in quite the last period of the probation.

There can be no escape from these absurdities by alleging that continuity and sameness in the form of the physical organization preserve the personal identity. The boy who bought the jack-knife, then lost the blades and had them replaced by new ones, then broke the handle and had it replaced, did not suppose he then possessed the knife first bought, because the size and style of it were preserved. A music-box is set running to the tune of "Sweet Home." Suppose that while the tune goes on there should be wrought in it, by some mysterious process, a displacement and replacement of particles precisely similar to that which takes place in the human body, until all the original particles should have passed out of it: would it then be the original box, because the tune continues without variation? Suppose all the eliminated particles to have dropped into a receptacle, and been reconstructed in a box giving forth the same tune: which now is the original box? To ask the question is to answer it. The identity of the first box was not transferred to the second by continuity of tune or organization. Neither can man's personal identity be transferred to the new particles which displace the old ones in his body by continuity of thought and feeling, if they are evolved from the physical organization like a tune from a musical instrument.

2. *Man's intuition of his own duality.* All the great schools of philosphy have based their

deduction upon intuitive cognitions, beliefs, and judgments of the mind; such as self-identity, causation, space, time, the infinite, the "me and the not me." These are seeds, roots, starting points of the mind, underived, independent, self-sufficient. "They rule the mind in its primitive energies of thought and belief." Argue, for instance, with an illiterate mind against the reality of an outward world; contend that all his ideas of it are from his senses, and these, all being in the mind, he knows of nothing out of his mind—no outward world. He cannot find the flaw in the chain of your logic, but he will not be bound to your conclusions. He will still say, "There is an outward world." Is he candid? Ought he to give up his intuition of "the not me" for your conclusion, because he cannot break your logic? Common sense replies no; for he must still rely on intuitions of self, and causation for the authority of your logic; and if in the first instance the intuition is not valid, how does it appear that it is in the second? Any philosophy which, in its ultimate conclusions, collides with these intuitive judgments, must go under as surely as the dory which collides with the steamer. As a means for the discovery of truth, philosophy and logic are indispensable. So is engineering for the discovery of the gold places; but when the precious metal is brought to the light, the rustic, as well as the engineer, can distinguish it from the dross. Doddridge, in writing his commentary, often appealed to the judgment of a humble woman in his parish, to test the accuracy of his exegesis.

Ask the more illiterate man if he believes that what in him thinks, loves, hates, desires, resolves, is the same as his bones, and the earth on which he treads, and he will laugh you to scorn for seriously asking such a question. You might as easily convince him that he walks on his head, or flies through the air, as that the pulp of his brain thinks.

So universal is this intuition that it has been one of the fixed data in all the schools from Anaxagoras to Hamilton, Epicureans and the Hobbesian wing of the Sensationalists alone excepted. With this inconsiderable exception, all the grand philosophies—the idealistic, the skeptical, the mystic, and the sensational—from 509 years B. C. to the present, have alike ranked it among the indestructible convictions of mankind. A fact of mental science which has stood the test of such a crucible, can hardly be jeered at as "a sublime absurdity," without an impeachment of the intelligence of the ages, which is ludicrous from its weakness.

3. *The absurdity of assuming that the mere organization of matter should evolve attributes which it did not originally possess.* Materialists admit that only certain forms of organized matter can think and feel. The admission is fatal to their theory, involving it in the paradox of producing something from nothing. If they claim for matter organized, properties not inherent in matter unorganized, it devolves on them to show *whence* those properties. Escape from the dilemma has been sought in a fancied analogy of the watch. "There is no time," it is said, "in the materials of which the watch is made;

yet when organized, it will indicate the hour, minute, and second." But in indicating the hour, minute, and second, does it develop a new *property*, or simply a function? Were not the elasticity in the spring, the adhesion in the chain, the hardness in the pivots, the smoothness in the dial, and the color in the ink of the figures, before what were organized? Is time in the watch in any other sense than that it performs certain mechanical functions from which inferences are drawn respecting the succession of "hours, minutes, and seconds?" To claim for matter organized in the watch any qualities it did not originally possess, is as palpably absurd as to claim for the granite of the milestones along the railroad new properties, because by them you count the miles you travel.

To say that the Creator may have developed out of the human organism the attributes of mind, though the act of doing it is inconceivable, is both to beg the question and aver an absurdity.

If mind is evolved from matter by organization, it is a phenomenon to be shown by the analysis of mind and matter; otherwise, all proof from that source fails.

To assume that the Creator, because omnipotent, may have evolved mind from matter, is as contradictory as to suppose him to develop the rule of three from a rose-bud, make a triangle weigh a pound, or create two mountains without a valley between them.

4. *The testimony of consciousness.* This is the source whence every fact in the philosophy of mind must be derived. Sir Wm. Hamilton defines it to be "the recognition, by the thinking subject, of its own acts or affections—the light which detects whatever comes into the mind." "It is the power by which mind is aware of its own states and activities," says Prof. C. S. Henry. "It is the sentinel which apprehends whatever comes into the mind," says Prof. H. Lummis, with equal pertinence and clearness.

All the late and high authorities now agree in affirming consciousness to be coextensive with the perceptions. The mind is conscious of every object which it perceives. This is the ground of certainty in our knowledge. The veracity of consciousness cannot be denied without *felo de se*. If you deny its veracity, you are conscious of denying, and hence assume its veracity in the act of denying it.

The testimony of consciousness to the duality of man is fourfold.

(1.) It testifies to the antithesis of mind and matter as clearly as it does to the antithesis of a moral virtue and a triangle. If matter, in any of its forms, and mind are identical, they must be so in their qualities. Consciousness cognizes, for example, in mind the qualities of perception and passion; in matter, resistance and extension. If these qualities are identical, they are interchangeable; and we may speak of the perception and passion of matter, and of the resistance and extension of mind. Let one converse in this way, and he would be thought a fit subject for the lunatic asylum. But if the essential qualities of mind and matter are antithetical, their respective subjects are absolutely separate entities.

(2.) Consciousness testifies to the presence of ideas in the mind which do not enter it through the senses. Ideas which strike the consciousness from the senses are all represented by the sensations, as the ideas of physical pain and pleasure. But how can ideas of the absolute, the infinite, space and duration, which are infinite in extent, be represented by sensations which are finite? How can a tree cast the shadow of a mountain, or a rill echo the thunder of Niagara?

Again, how can we conceive ideas of good and evil to be represented by the sensations? "By regarding them as synonymous with pleasure and pain," said Hobbes; and thus struck at the foundation of morals and religion. To recoil from such infidelity is to abandon the materialistic origin of religious ideas.

If, then, there are ideas in the mind not derived from the senses, they must have had their origin in an entity distinct from the body.

(3.) Consciousness testifies to being itself already in the mind when the sensations enter it. I strike my body, and a sensation is produced. I am conscious of it because I feel it; if I did not feel it, there would be no sensation. There are, then, in this experience, three things: (*a.*) The sensation; (*b.*) The cognition of it; (*c.*) The subject which cognizes it. But the sensation is not the consciousness, for it is the object of cognition. The cognition is not the consciousness any more than the act of seeing is the eye. The subject which cognizes, then, must be the consciousness. But the subject which cognizes must be logically antecedent to the thing cognized. If, then, consciousness is logically antecedent to sensation, it does not originate in it, and is independent of it.

(4.) Consciousness testifies to an original causative power in the mind, which cannot be predicated of the sensations. I am conscious of choosing, and of power not to choose—of willing, and of power not to will. Not so with the sensations. If I cut my hand, the sensation of pain will continue, with no power to arrest it. I am conscious of feeling it, with the consciousness of not being able not to feel it. But when I act, it is with the consciousness of power not to act.

These facts make the distinction between mind and the physical organization so broad and clear that it seems unnecessary to enlarge further upon it.

5. *The veracity of the Creator.* He alone is responsible for the validity of every belief which arises necessarily in the mind. I cannot avoid the belief that I exist in space. If this belief is not valid, my existence is a cheat. I have, for instance, a conscience which necessitates belief in the reality of moral distinctions. If those distinctions are a chimera, then He who endowed me with the conscience whence that belief of necessity springs, is subjecting me to a life-long deception. In like manner does the veracity of God guarantee validity to the belief in the duality of man—an intuition of which the common mind cannot dispossess itself.

That the intuitive nature of this belief has been denied does not invalidate the argument drawn from it, for this is true of all the other intuitions. Men have denied the existence of self, of the outer world, of the infinite, the absolute, space, duration, good and evil, causation. At intervals, along the path of speculative thought, these periodic land-slides of scholastic rubbish have overslaughed the deeper life of the soul; but its germinant forces have sprung up through and around them, like Alpine flowers amid the glaciers, attesting a deathless vitality despite the superincumbent congelations. These checks, if such they deserve to be called, to the true philosophy, only show it the more clearly to be the very essence of human thinking, which, like Milton's angels,

> "Vital in every part,
> Cannot but by annihilation die."

This argument has cumulative force from the assurance of the dying saint that he is about "to depart and be with Christ," and that "to die is gain." After discounting all that Materialists can fairly claim as the result of what they allege to be false teachings upon this subject, careful observation will discover in these experiences a large margin left for a spontaneity, springing, not from theoretical belief, but from the revelation (uncovering) of Christ in the soul. It is the bubbling up of a fountain within, having its natural outgushing in the sweet symphony of Rowland Hill,

> "This I do find, we two are so joined,
> He'll not live in glory, and leave me behind."

Behind, in a myriad ages of unconsciousness!—behind, to be scattered to the winds with the dust of the poor body! Perish the thought! No such chasm can mar the symmetry of the Divine plan, whose crowning perfection should be the fruition of intuitional hopes, matured and intensified in proportion to the conformity of their subject to the spirit and precepts of that plan. To affirm such an absurdity is to cast a baleful shadow over the whole of experimental Christianity.

6. *The Phenomena of death.* If the soul is a

part of the body, is it not in the body at what is called death? If so, is the body dead? Ought it to be buried? Is not the person only asleep, and as truly liable to awake as one who sleeps for the night? If the soul is the result of organization, it must continue in the body while the organization remains unimpaired. But at the instant of death no change occurs in the organization of the body; there is simply a cessation of its functions. Anatomical examination finds every part perfect as before the breath left the body. A live coal placed upon a stone parts with its caloric and changes its color, but not its organization. To assume a change of bodily organization because of the cessations of bodily functions, when physiological facts do not show it, is to beg the question.

If the soul remains in the body at death, where is it in the case of the martyrs whose bodies were burned and scattered to the four quarters of the globe? If it is out of the body, is it not immaterial? If it is neither in the body nor out of it, is it not annihilated? And, therefore, is it not a false use of words to talk of the sleep of the soul at death? As well affirm the sleep of a soul before it begins to exist, as after it has ceased to exist.

It is unnecessary to follow this line of thought further. The simple facts adduced, as clearly reveal a twofold nature in man as the steamer plowing the sea shows a joint force of propulsion and resistance.

The following objections are urged:

1. *No one has ever seen man otherwise than as a unit.* That is, No one by his senses has seen an immaterial nature in man; therefore he has none. No one by his senses has seen God, and is there therefore no God? But it is not true that no one has, by his *consciousness*, seen —cognized—man otherwise than as a unit.

2. *If there be a soul in man distinct from the body, define it.* This is easily done. The soul is indivisible, imponderable; it exists in time and space, and possesses conative, emotional, and cognitive powers. Can body be any more clearly defined than can soul?

3. *If no one has seen the soul, it is presumption to say that it exists.* If "no man has seen God at any time," is it presumption to say that he exists?

4. *If man has an immaterial soul, where did he get it? If immediately from God, God is the immediate author of his innate depravity. If from the parent, the parent's soul is divisible.*

The soul comes from God in no other sense than does the body. Both are the result of God's established economy. If the depravity is alleged, the difficulty is not avoided by shifting depravity from the soul to the body, since both alike spring from an economy of which God is the author.

But the presumption is, that the soul, with the body, proceeds from the parent. The only objection urged against this is, that it is a contradiction, since the soul is defined to be indivisible. Yet is not God indivisible? And is it, therefore, a contradiction to say that our first parents came immediately from him?

If a single instance can be adduced of the

creation of an entity by a soul, then the contradiction charged upon the presumption that the soul creates, without dividing itself, vanishes. Now if I throw a ball, it will go on forever, if it meet with no resistance. Why? Because it possesses a certain *quantum* of force which I have imparted to it. Yet my force is not diminished by what I have imparted to the ball. Have I not, then, created an entity without dividing myself? But if I have created one entity without dividing myself, I may another, for aught that appears in the nature of the case. Thus does this alleged contradiction vanish like a bubble at the touch, leaving the presumption in favor of the procreation of the soul. Where is there proof to the contrary?

5. *If the soul is immaterial, it ought to remember when it became united with the body.* For a reason just as conclusive, it ought, if material, to remember when it was dislodged from the body of the parent. Has it such a recollection?

6. *If the soul is immaterial, it should be logi-*

cally conscious of its existence prior to its union with the body. For a similar reason, if the soul is material, it should be conscious of its existence at the moment of procreation. It is as easy to affirm the latter as the former.

7. *If the soul is immaterial, it should know its own existence without being apprised of it by the senses.* Certainly; and this is just what it does know. It is only by first knowing its own existence that it can know that it has sensations. It knows it has physical pleasure and pain because it feels them; and knows it feels them because there is a subject which feels, and which is not the feelings or sensations themselves. Chronologically, the consciousness may be coetaneous with the sensations; but logically, it must ever be antecedent to them.

8. *If consciousness be the fruit of the senses, how can it be shown to be an attribute of an immaterial entity?* If by this is meant that the senses are the *cause* of consciousness, the affirmation is denied. As already shown, conscious-

ness is in the mind antecedent to the sensations. If it is simply meant that the senses *occasion* the acts of consciousness, there is no more difficulty in the case than that these objections should occasion my attempt to answer them.

9. *If the soul cognizes its existence only through the senses, how can its existence as a separate entity be affirmed?* It is not true that the soul cognizes its existence only through the senses. "It starts with a knowledge of itself," says Sir Wm. Hamilton. The sensations are an occasion of its development: but it is aware of its own existence antecedent to the sensations, otherwise their presence could not be perceived. If perceived, there must be a perceiver, and the perceiving must be logically antecedent to the thing perceived.

10. *If the soul does not depend upon organized matter for its attributes, why should it ever be unconscious of its own being?* If the soul does depend upon organized matter for its attributes, why should it ever lose self-consciousness in sleep, so long as the organization re-

mains unchanged? The latter case is just as inexplicable as the former. But if it is intended to affirm that the suspension of the senses causes a suspension of the consciousness, the affirmation is denied, and the burden of proof falls upon him who makes it.

The consciousness of self may be diverted. The boy chasing the butterfly is not for the moment conscious of himself; but his consciousness is not therefore suspended, it is only directed to another object. The martyrs were enwrapped in such a blaze of glory as not to be conscious of the crisping of their flesh at the stake, but it was because they were conscious of something else.

The evidence is strong that the consciousness is never suspended. If it is, how could a sensation ever arouse it? I strike my hand—no sensation is produced unless I feel it; but if I feel it, there is something in me antecedently awake which feels, otherwise the impact would not be a sensation.

We recall many of the mental activities of a

state of sleep. Is not the presumption strong that if the memory were perfect, activities filling every moment of sleep would be recalled? To infer that there were none except such as are recalled is as absurd as to infer that there were no activities in one's boyhood except such as he can recall.

A person goes to sleep charging himself to wake at a given hour, and wakes when the hour arrives. Does not his consciousness retain the charge committed to it? The faithful nurse sleeps so soundly that the rattle of the wheels upon the pavement does not disturb her, but the first rustle of the patient brings her instantly to her feet. Does not her consciousness watch the patient? A ball struck the head of an officer in the Crimea when giving a command, and left him in a state of insensibility. On recovering from it, his first mental act was to finish giving the command. Did not his consciousness retain the thought during the interval of physical insensibility?

With these strong facts supporting the continuity of consciousness, its suspension should not be assumed, as in this objection, without proof.

11. *The argument for the twofold nature of man, based on the alleged antithesis of mind and matter, proves the twofold nature of beasts.* Admitted. What then? They may or may not be immortal. That they have a degree of intelligence no one will deny.

12. *A second childhood obtains in old age.* If this is because the mind is material, and comes under the same law of decay which is inherent in the body, then its imbecility ought invariably to commence at the period when the waste of the body exceeds the supply, at the age of forty or fifty years. If a single exception to this can be adduced, it is sufficient to show that mind is not under the control of physical law, as is the body, and consequently is not a part of the body.

If a single instance could be adduced in which a feather does not obey the law of gravitation, it would break the universality of that law, and reverse the whole theory of the cosmos. But not only is there one instance in which the vigor of the mind is not affected by the decay of the body; the instances are so universal that their converse is the rare exception. The greatest intellectual vigor of which history boasts has been developed after the body had become decrepit with age and disease. This no one will deny; and it at once and forever enthrones mind over physical law, and establishes its immortality.

It must be obvious that the materialism which just now clamors for the sanctions of the Bible and the honor of the Christian name, logically strikes at the foundation of all morals and religion. If the soul is material it must be absolutely under the control of physical law, and be incapable of obedience to any other. There can be no exception to this more than there can be to the fact that water seeks an equilibrium, or that a stone drops to the earth. A material substance must as inevitably remain subject to material law as a galley-slave to the motions of the boat to which he is chained. To allege that mind, as a part of the body, can obey moral law, is as unthinkable as that a body can occupy two points in space at the same time. Thus reasoned Hobbes from premises furnished him by the sensational philosophy, and with a logical consistency which sent a tremor throughout Christendom proclaimed virtue and vice to be mere figures of speech.

Again, if all our ideas are derived from the sensations, by what means can we have any idea of that which is not material? This is the question which Hume asked in vain to have Locke answer from his premises. Hume accepted the logical consequences of his master's teachings, and plunged into the maelstrom of religious skepticism. Locke heard the roar of the vortex, gave up philosophy, and threw himself upon Revelation, which was his only surety for any thing beyond the material world; his moral consistency overmatched his philosophy and rescued him. Hobbes and Hume only followed out with irrefragable logic the sequences of premises which the Materialists of the present time are again seeking to consecrate at the shrine of religion. Let them be met at the threshold with the facts of a second Psychology.

> "Hold thou the good; define it well,
> For fear divine Philosophy
> Should push beyond her mark, and be
> Procuress to the lords of hell."

THE END.

Choice Books for Youth,

PUBLISHED BY NELSON & PHILLIPS,

805 BROADWAY, N. Y.

William the Taciturn.
Translated by J. P. LACROIX. From the French of L. ABELOUS. Two Illustrations.............. $1 25

Thomas Chalmers.
A Biographical Study. By JAMES DODD. Large 16mo.. 1 50

Word of God Opened.
By B. K. PEIRCE. Large 16mo................. 1 25

Christian Maiden.
Memorials of Eliza Hessel. With a Portrait. By JOSHUA PRIESTLEY.......................... 1 25

Stories and Pictures from Church History.
For Young People. Illustrated. Large 16mo.. 1 25

Agnes Morton's Trial,
And the Young Governess. By Mrs. E. N. JANVIER. Large 16mo......................... 1 25

Life of Oliver Cromwell.
By CHARLES ADAMS, D.D. 16mo............. 1 25

Earth and its Wonders.
By CHARLES ADAMS, D.D. 16mo............. 1 25

Edith Vernon's Life-Work.
Large 16mo. Illustrated...................... 1 25

Exiles in Babylon.
By A. L. O. E. Illustrated.................... 1 00

Lindsay Lee and his Friends.

A Story for the Time. Large 16mo............ $0 75

Gustavus Adolphus,

The Hero of the Reformation. From the French of L. Abelous. By Mrs. C. A. Lacroix. Illustrated. Large 16mo.......................... 1 00

Heroine of the White Nile;

Or, What a Woman Did and Dared. A Sketch of the Remarkable Travels and Experiences of Miss Alexandrine Tinné. By Prof. William Wells. Illustrated. Large 16mo............. 1 00

Memoir of Washington Irving.

With Selections from his Works, and Criticisms. By Charles Adams, D.D. Large 16mo........ 1 25

Itinerant Side;

Or, Pictures of Life in the Itinerancy. With Engravings.................................... 1 00

Life of Dr. Samuel Johnson.

By C. Adams, D.D. Large 16mo............... 1 25

Lady Huntingdon Portrayed.

Including Brief Sketches of some of her Friends and Colaborers. By the Author of "The Missionary Teacher," "Sketches of Mission Life," etc. 1 25

Ministering Children.

A Story showing how even a Child may be as a Ministering Angel of Love to the Poor and Sorrowful. Illustrated............................ 1 50

Lives made Sublime by Faith and Works.

Large 16mo. Illustrated...................... 1 50

My Sister Margaret.

A Temperance Story. Four Illustrations. By Mrs. C. M. Edwards........................... 1 25

Palissy the Potter;

Or, the Huguenot, Artist, and Martyr. A True Narrative. By C. L. Brightwell. Illustrated. 1 25

Footprints of Roger Williams.

By Rev. Z. A. Mudge. Large 16mo............ $1 25

Path of Life.

By D. Wise, D.D. Large 16mo................ 1 00
Gilt Edge.................................. 1 30

The Ministry of Life.

By Maria Louisa Charlesworth, Author of "Ministering Children," etc. With Illustrations 1 25

Pleasant Pathways;

Or, Persuasives to Early Piety. By Daniel Wise, D.D. Steel Engravings................. 1 25

The Poet Preacher:

A Brief Memorial of Charles Wesley, the Eminent Preacher and Poet. By Charles Adams. Illustrated.. 1 00

The Stony Road.

A Scottish Story from Real Life. Large 16mo.. 0 85

Pillars of Truth.

A Series of Sermons on the Decalogue. By E. O. Haven, D.D............................... 1 25

The Rainbow Side.

A Sequel to "The Itinerant." By Mrs. C. M. Edwards. With Four Illustrations........... 1 25

The Shepherd King;

Or, a Sick Minister's Lectures on the Shepherd of Bethlehem, and the Blessing that followed Them. By A. L. O. E., Authoress of the "Young Pilgrim," "The Roby Family," etc. Illustrated. 1 25

Trials of an Inventor:

Life and Discoveries of Charles Goodyear. Large 16mo....................................... 1 25

Views from Plymouth Rock.

By Z. A. Mudge. With Six Illustrations. Large 16mo....................................... 1 50

Words that Shook the World;

Or, Martin Luther his own Biographer. Being Pictures of the Great Reformer, sketched mainly from his own Sayings. By CHARLES ADAMS. Illustrated $1 25

Young Lady's Counselor.

By D. WISE, D.D. Large 16mo 1 00
Gilt Edge 1 30

Young Man's Counselor.

By D. WISE, D.D. Large 16mo 1 00
Gilt Edge 1 30

Six Years in India.

By MR. HUMPHREYS 1 25

Young Shetlander and his Home.

Being a Biographical Sketch of Young Thomas Edmonston, the Naturalist, and an Interesting Account of the Shetland Islands. By B. K. PEIRCE, D.D. Illustrated. Large 16mo 1 25

Children of Lake Huron;

Or, the Cousins at Cloverley. 16mo 1 25

Dora Hamilton;

Or, Sunshine and Shadow. Six Illustrations. 16mo 0 90

Discipline of Alice Lee.

A Truthful Temperance Story. Illustrated. 16mo 1 00

Suzanna De L'Orme.

A Story of Huguenot Times. Large 16mo 1 25

The Christian Statesman.

A Portraiture of Sir Thomas Fowell Buxton. By Z. A. MUDGE 1 25

The Forest Boy.

A Sketch of the Life of Abraham Lincoln. By Z. A. MUDGE. Large 16mo 1 25